*To Averleigh,
with Furry Love!
Doris A. Plough*

My Dog Molly
Doris A. Plough

Copyright © 2018 Doris A. Plough.

All rights reserved. No part of this book may be used or reproduced by any means, graphic, electronic, or mechanical, including photocopying, recording, taping or by any information storage retrieval system without the written permission of the author except in the case of brief quotations embodied in critical articles and reviews.

This book is a work of non-fiction. Unless otherwise noted, the author and the publisher make no explicit guarantees as to the accuracy of the information contained in this book and in some cases, names of people and places have been altered to protect their privacy.

Balboa Press books may be ordered through booksellers or by contacting:

Balboa Press
A Division of Hay House
1663 Liberty Drive
Bloomington, IN 47403
www.balboapress.com
1 (877) 407-4847

Because of the dynamic nature of the Internet, any web addresses or links contained in this book may have changed since publication and may no longer be valid. The views expressed in this work are solely those of the author and do not necessarily reflect the views of the publisher, and the publisher hereby disclaims any responsibility for them.

Any people depicted in stock imagery provided by Getty Images are models, and such images are being used for illustrative purposes only.
Certain stock imagery © Getty Images.

ISBN: 978-1-9822-0840-0 (sc)
ISBN: 978-1-9822-0839-4 (e)

Print information available on the last page.

Balboa Press rev. date: 08/15/2018

To Ms. Averleigh ~ And her wonderful mommy Angelia ~ I hope you enjoy Ms. Clough's book. She loves her doggies, and she also loved your photo, the one with you wearing glasses, Ms. Averleigh — she also loves your name. I love you both, and always will.
Great Grandmother Patty Prell
12-25-2018

My Dog Molly

Does anyone know, does anyone care
    Where you go or how you fare,
Whether your happy or,
    Whether you are blue,
It matters to me dear friend,
    Cause I Love YOU ....

 Let me begin by telling you a story about a beautiful dog, my dog named Molly. It is not a sad story, but yet one of devoted love between a dog and her mistress.

It was a lovely fall day when we took a drive to Palmdale to pick up a small Westie puppy. When we drove up to the yard the first thing I saw was a small white face peering through the fence. I thought to myself...' how will she ever grow into her ears...as they seemed much too big for her head??? Yet her big brown eyes looked back at me in such a way that it was love at first sight, and I thought she was perhaps the most precious dog in the whole world.

We named her Molly, and she became the companion of our other West Highland, Mr. Mcgreagor. She grew into a beautiful dog, and yes, she grew into her ears. With soft brown eyes and a tender loving disposition. She loved to do her high-fives, where she would stand on her hind legs and reach out her front paws to you.!! She would do this for hours on end, if you would let her.

The background of the West Highland Terrier or Westies as they are called have their origin in Scotland many centuries ago. They were primarily used as a hunting dog to go into holes in the ground to flush out small game. Despite their hunting instincts, they are proud, friendly and intelligent. They were not always white, but reddish brown in color. Because of a hunting accident were the dog was mistaken for another animal, thereafter only pure white dogs were breed. However this took years to accomplish. Thus we have the Westie as we know it today, a proud lovable companion.

We took the dogs most everywhere with us, as they were our family. While Mr. Mcgreagor, boy like had a tendency for mischievous behavior [he ran away three times] Molly was always the good girl.

We had a small travel trailer which we would hook up to the big white truck, load the dogs in the back section of the cab and off we would go on our adventures. One of our favorite places to go was a park south of San Diego, which overlooked the ocean.

The dogs loved to travel, and when we pulled into the gate of the park, they knew somehow that their adventures were about to begin. They especially loved sitting outside and greeting all the other dogs that passed by who wanted to say....HELLO!!! One time however Mr. Mcgreagor slipped his leash and wandered down to another trailer and asked if he could come in?? The next thing we knew I heard a voice calling out...does anybody know who this Westie belongs too?????

Of course we retrieved him, apologized for his behavior and chalked it up to him just being...Mr. Mcgreagor, our escape artist.

Our adventures in the trailer took us many places, and the dogs always went with us. It was a joy and a pleasure to function as a dog loving family.

Mcgreagor, however passed on to doggie heaven, and we quickly got a new pal for Molly, as she was pining away for her lost friend. Our new edition was a small Carine terrier, who we named Mandy. A bundle of carmel colored fir, she had boundless energy, yet she and Molly soon became great pals, and companions in travel.

Again our days of travel were full and happy ones, although Mandy seemed to hog all the attention everywhere we went, for she was so full of life. Molly always seemed to stand back and let her have all the glory, for by this time she too was getting along in years.

It was in the summer of her 12th year that one evening as we were relaxing watching a movie on t.v. that Mandy began a loud shrill bark. The next thing I knew the whole bed began to shake, and Molly was jerking and shaking violently. It seemed to last an eternity, yet in reality it was probably a few seconds.

I took her in my arms, after the shaking subsided, and tried to comfort her in a calm voice, she was indeed having a seizure. {The dictionary describes a seizure as a violent attack] However when seizures occur the dog may appear to be frightened or dazed, or may hide or reach out for attention. Once the seizure has began, the dog will usually fall on its side, and become very stiff. These seizures usually last between 30 and 90 seconds.

This is the same thing that happens to some people, the only diffence being that with animals there is no way to let them know what is happening to them. We consulted our Vet, who put her on medications for seizures, but without costly testing and putting her thru much, all we could hope for was a good result from the medication.!!!

It is ½ year later and she still suffers from seizers on occasion. When this happens, I try to hold her and comfort her, just like I would a child!! She always looks up a me with those big brown eyes and I realize how very hard this is for all of us, but I think she knows I am trying to help her.

The moral to this story is that perhaps life deals all of god's children, be it animal or human some bad blows in the course of a lifetime. Perhaps YOU know of someone with some disabilities. If so, reach out to them with love and support in any way you can, and your kindness and love will come back to you in many ways!

This story is a tribute to a brave
little dog named MOLLY!!!
By Doris A. Plough

... Molly & Mandy with their doggie mother.... Doris

My Dog Molly is a tribute to a loving friend and companion also a thoughtful reminder to those with special needs --

Doris A. Plough is a Disney trained artist with 50 years experience in the animation industry. She has worked in nearly all of the major studios... however her great love of animals is reflected in this story. A little white dog with a special problem touched her heart completely. So much so that her story needed to be told!

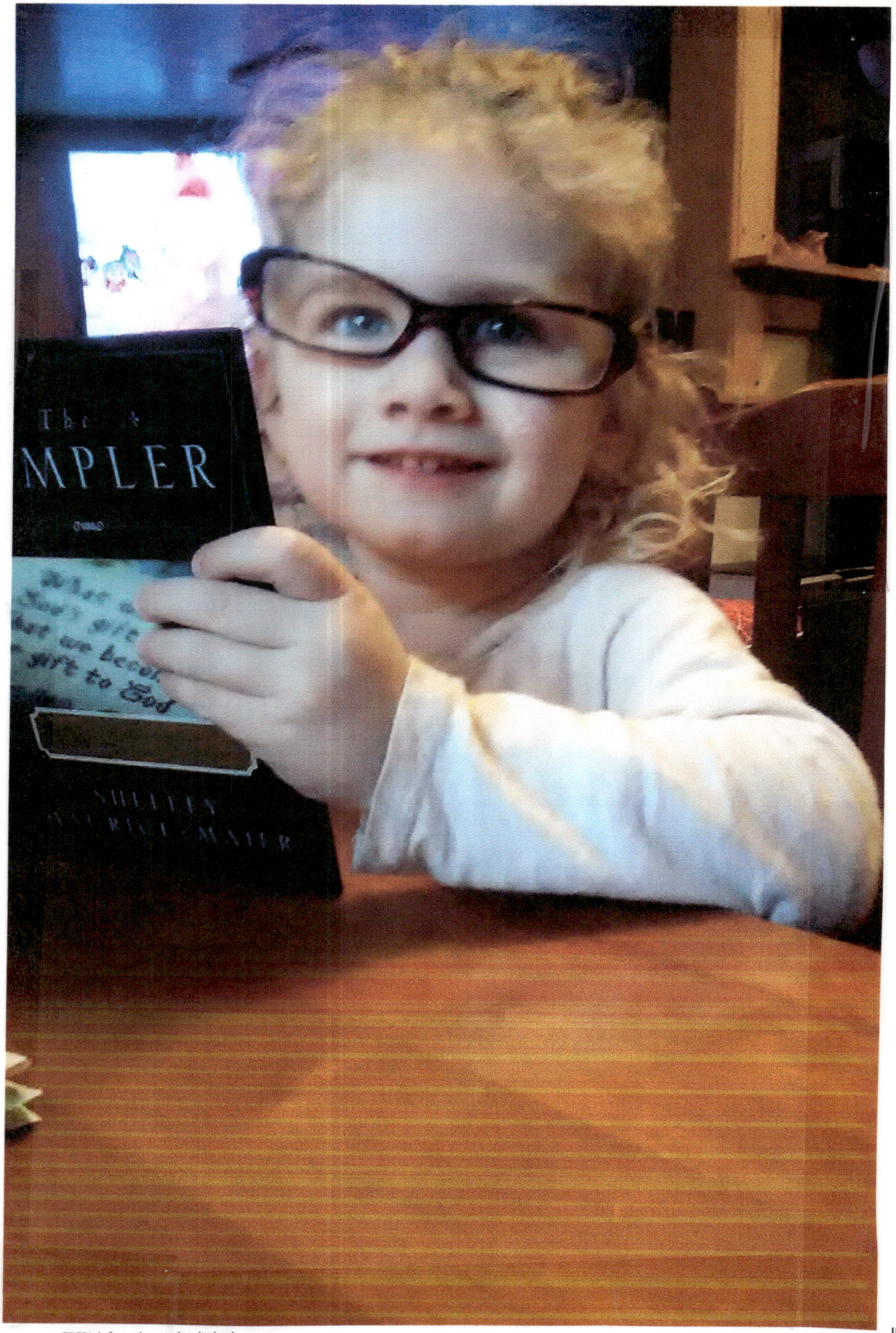

CPSIA information can be obtained
at www.ICGtesting.com
Printed in the USA
BVHW02s0829150918
527591BV00012B/104/P

9 781982 208400